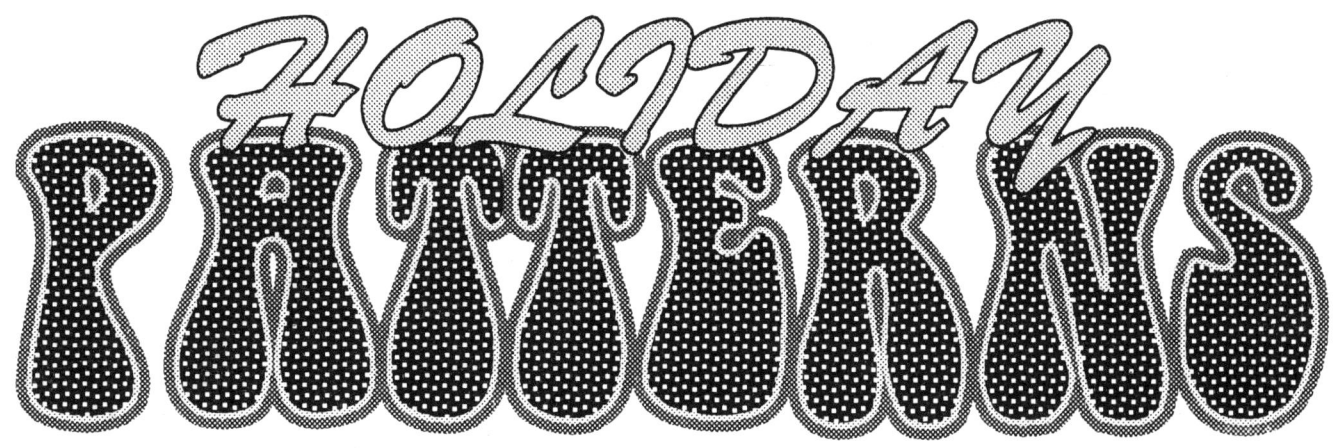

Written by	Linda Milliken
Cover design by	Mary Jo Keller Linda Milliken
Illustrated by	Dana Solomon Barb Lorseyedi

Reproducible for classroom use only.
Not for use by an entire school or school system.

© **Edupress** Revised 1995 • P.O. Box 883 • Dana Point, CA 92629

ISBN 1-56472-058-6

Leaf

Art: On white drawing paper, trace 4 leaves. Paint each to show a season. Red, yellow or orange for fall, brown for winter, yellow and green for spring and summer.

OR make a large group mural, tracing leaves and painting them the appropriate colors for the season.

Large motor development: *Teacher task—* Cut enough leaves to make a pile. Scatter the leaves in a cleared classroom space. Provide rakes and ask the children to rake the leaves into a pile.

Small motor development: Now work in pairs, one holding a paper trash bag and the other picking the leaves from the pile and putting them carefully in the bag. Scatter the leaves again and repeat, exchanging roles.

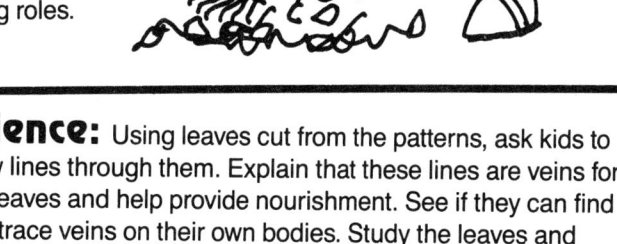

Science: Using leaves cut from the patterns, ask kids to draw lines through them. Explain that these lines are veins for the leaves and help provide nourishment. See if they can find and trace veins on their own bodies. Study the leaves and trace the veins too.

Letter or number recognition: Write a letter or number on each leaf. Be sure there are duplications. Scatter the leaves. Hunt for the leaves with the letter "L" etc.

Comparing: Start a leaf collection. Ask children to collect leaves at home and bring them to class. Go on a group walk to add to your collection. Compare the kinds of leaves. How many different ones can you find? Make a chart.

Categorizing: Use the class leaf collection for developing categorizing skills. Ask kids to help group the leaves by size, color and shape.

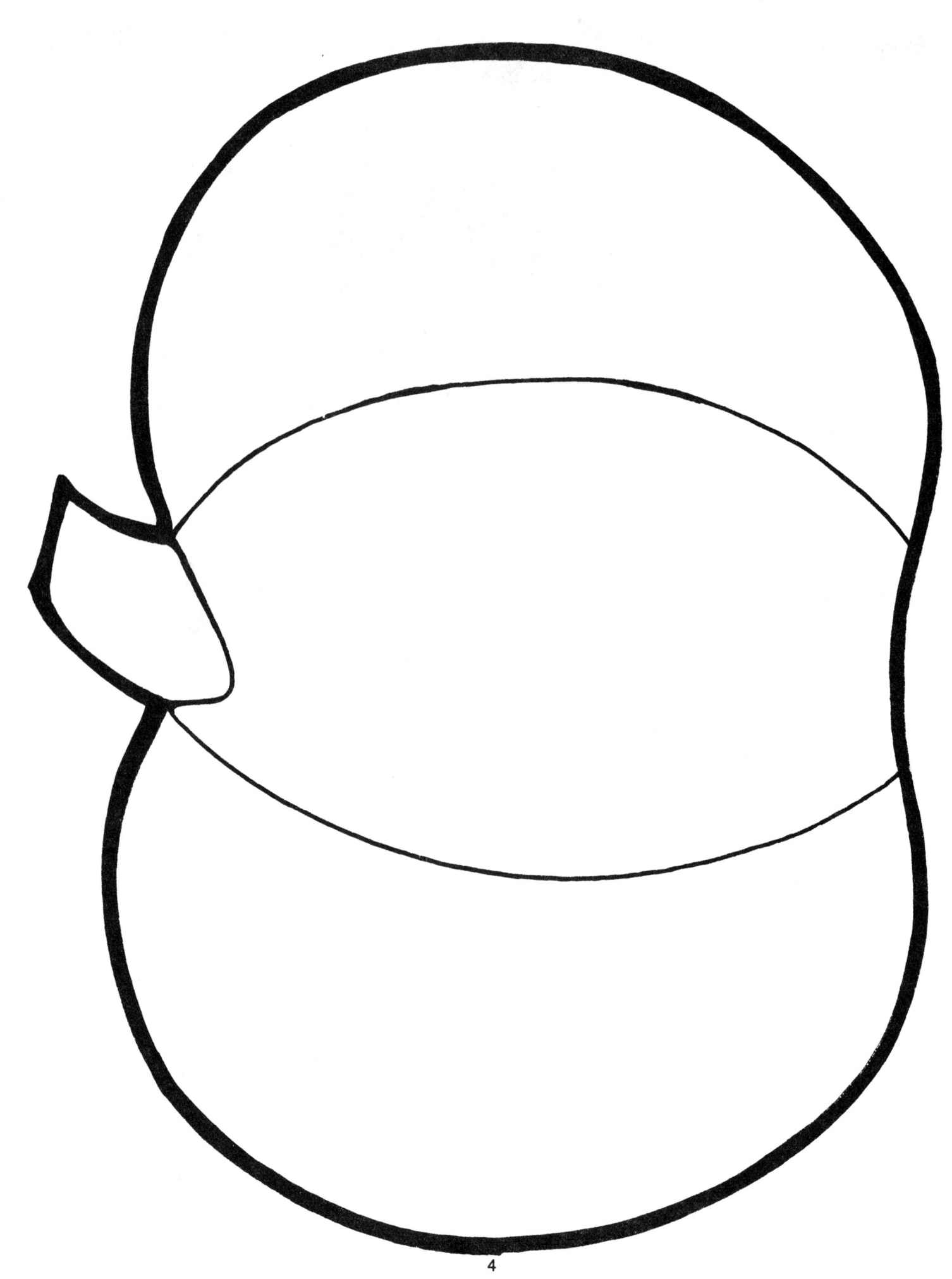

Pumpkin

Art: Turn cut out pumpkins into houses by adding doors, windows, and chimneys using glued paper scraps. Create a pumpkin city by mounting the pumpkins on butcher paper. Kids can paint streets and trees.

Language development: Each child paints a jack-o-lantern face on an orange paper pumpkin. Put word headings on the wall—happy, sad, scary, spooky, and so on. After the jack-o-lantern paint has dried show each one to the group. Decide which heading the jack-o-lantern should go under and mount it on the wall.

Verbal skills, self-expression: Using the jack-o-lanterns on the wall as motivators talk about what might make the pumpkins feel happy, sad, scared, etc.

Science: Start a real pumpkin patch either in pots or in the ground outside your classroom. Plant pumpkin seeds, water daily. Be sure to put a large paper pumpkin labeled *Pumpkin Patch* near the garden!

Small motor development: Glue real pumpkin seeds "inside" the pumpkin pattern. This takes real practice using the thumb and forefinger!

Counting: Count the number of seeds glued inside each pumpkin. Then put seeds in a pile and count them, too!

Math: Bring a scale and several pumpkins of varying size to class. Ask the children which pumpkin they think will weigh the most, the least, etc. Now take turns putting the pumpkins on the scale and recording their weights.

Ghost

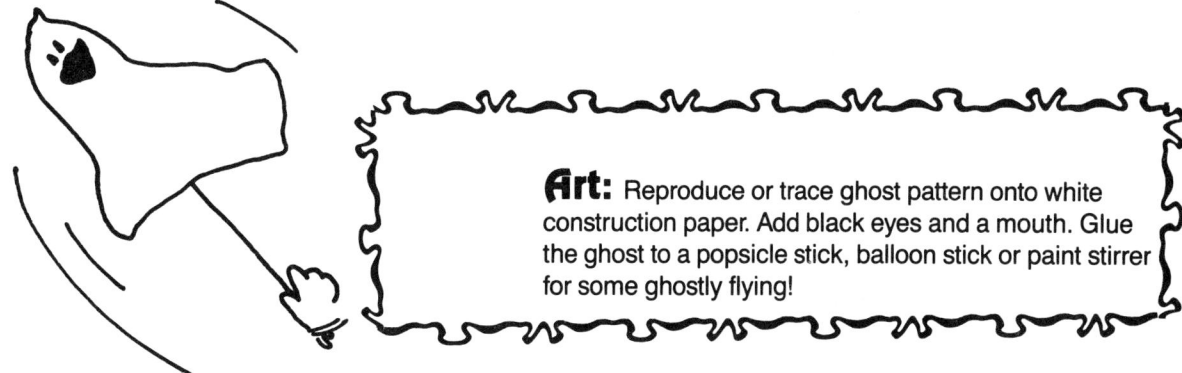

Art: Reproduce or trace ghost pattern onto white construction paper. Add black eyes and a mouth. Glue the ghost to a popsicle stick, balloon stick or paint stirrer for some ghostly flying!

Listening skills: Read the ghost story below. Each time the children hear the word "ghost" they put their ghost-on-a-stick (see ART above) in the air and say "boo."

One dark Halloween night we went for a walk in GHOST city. We were looking for GHOSTS. But, as you know, GHOSTS are hard to find because they cannot be seen. Then we felt a quiet breeze go past our heads. "Hush," I said, "it may be a GHOST!" We listened for a while and looked carefully for a GHOST. We never did see one. Do you believe in GHOSTS? Look! There's one right in front of you!

Counting, ordinal numbers: Line five children in a row with their stick-ghosts in front of them. Recite the poem. Each child in the row will say their own part, then all get up and move to make room for the next group of five.

Five little ghosts sitting on a gate.
The first one said, "My, it's getting late."
The second one said, "There are witches in the air."
The third one said, "We don't care."
The fourth one said, "Let's run, let's run."
The fifth one said, "It's only Halloween fun."
Whoo went the wind, out went the lights.
Those five little ghosts ran fast out of sight.

Small motor development: *Teacher task*—Using the pattern, cut several ghosts from cardboard. Put a piece of waxed paper over white construction paper then the cardboard ghost on top of that. Ask kids to trace around the pattern. Remove pattern and waxed paper. Paint a thin pastel watercolor wash over the construction paper. A ghost should appear!

Cooking: Make some ghostly goodies. Spread a graham cracker with peanut butter. Then spread marshmallow whip on top. The kids can do this, depending on age.

Turkey

Art: Reproduce pattern on white construction paper. Fingerpaint turkey and cut it out. Make a barnyard scene on white butcher paper. Glue the turkeys to the scene. Mount the mural on the wall.

Listening skills: Read the turkey story below. Each time a child hears the word "turkey" he holds up his turkey and says "gobble-gobble."

There was lots of noise in the barnyard! All the TURKEYS were running in circles. What could the matter be? What was upsetting the TURKEYS? I went to investigate. I walked as carefully as I could through the TURKEYS. I looked everywhere for a clue. Finally I saw my little sister sitting in the middle of all the TURKEYS. She had a big basket of food for the TURKEYS. They were enjoying a TURKEY feast!

Nutrition: Cut out magazine pictures showing what you might like to eat for a Thankgiving feast. Glue the pictures around the turkey on a large piece of construction paper.

Large motor development: Go outside and learn to trot. Then have some turkey trot races.

Letter or number recognition:
Teacher task—Use the pattern to cut a flannel turkey. Cut flannel feathers and write a number or letter on each. Ask a child to find a feather with a particular number or letter and attach it to the turkey on the flannel board.

Color recognition: *Teacher task*—cut 5 colored feathers and one turkey for each child. Cut each feather a different color, one each of red, blue, orange, green and yellow. Instruct the children to glue the red feather to the turkey. Check for correctness. Then proceed to another color until all have been glued to the turkey.

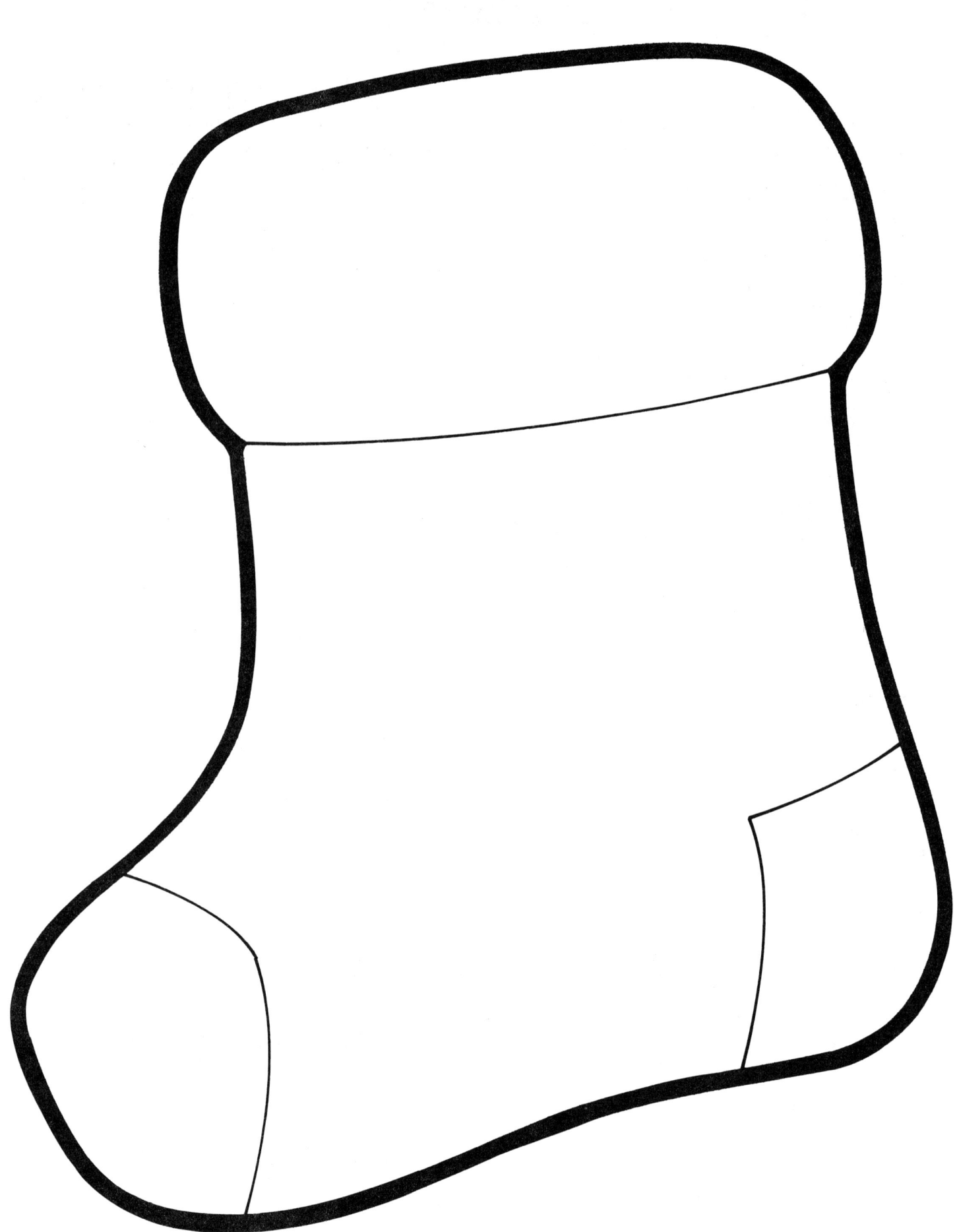

Stocking

Art: Using the pattern reproduce or trace two stockings. Cut out the two stockings and paint, color or decorate. Staple the stockings together.

Bulletin board: Cut rectangular shapes from red construction paper. Sponge paint black around the edges. (Kids can do this!) Mount the rectangles to resemble a fireplace (see illustration). Hang the stockings by the chimney. Write each child's name either on or over the stocking.

Oral expression: "Fill" each stocking with a magazine picture. Ask the children to discover what is in their stocking and tell the others about it.

Letter recognition: Cut a paper letter for each letter of the alphabet. Put a different letter in each stocking. When children arrive in the morning they will pick their letter out of the stocking and pin it on. Throughout the day ask them to identify their letter or the letter another person is wearing. Collect the letters before children go home and fill the stockings again.

This can be varied for number recognition and beginning letter sounds.

Motor skill development: Divide into teams for a fun-filled "sock hop". Provide each team wtih a pair of large socks. Kids take off their own shoes and socks. At a starting signal, the first person has to put on both stockings, hop to a line and back, take the stockings off again and pass them to the next person who repeats the task. Winning team is first one done!

Comparing sizes: Brainstorm and create a list of things, anything! Now go back over the list. Which items would be small enough to fit in your stockings? Which items would be too big?

Creative thinking: What would you like to find in your stocking?

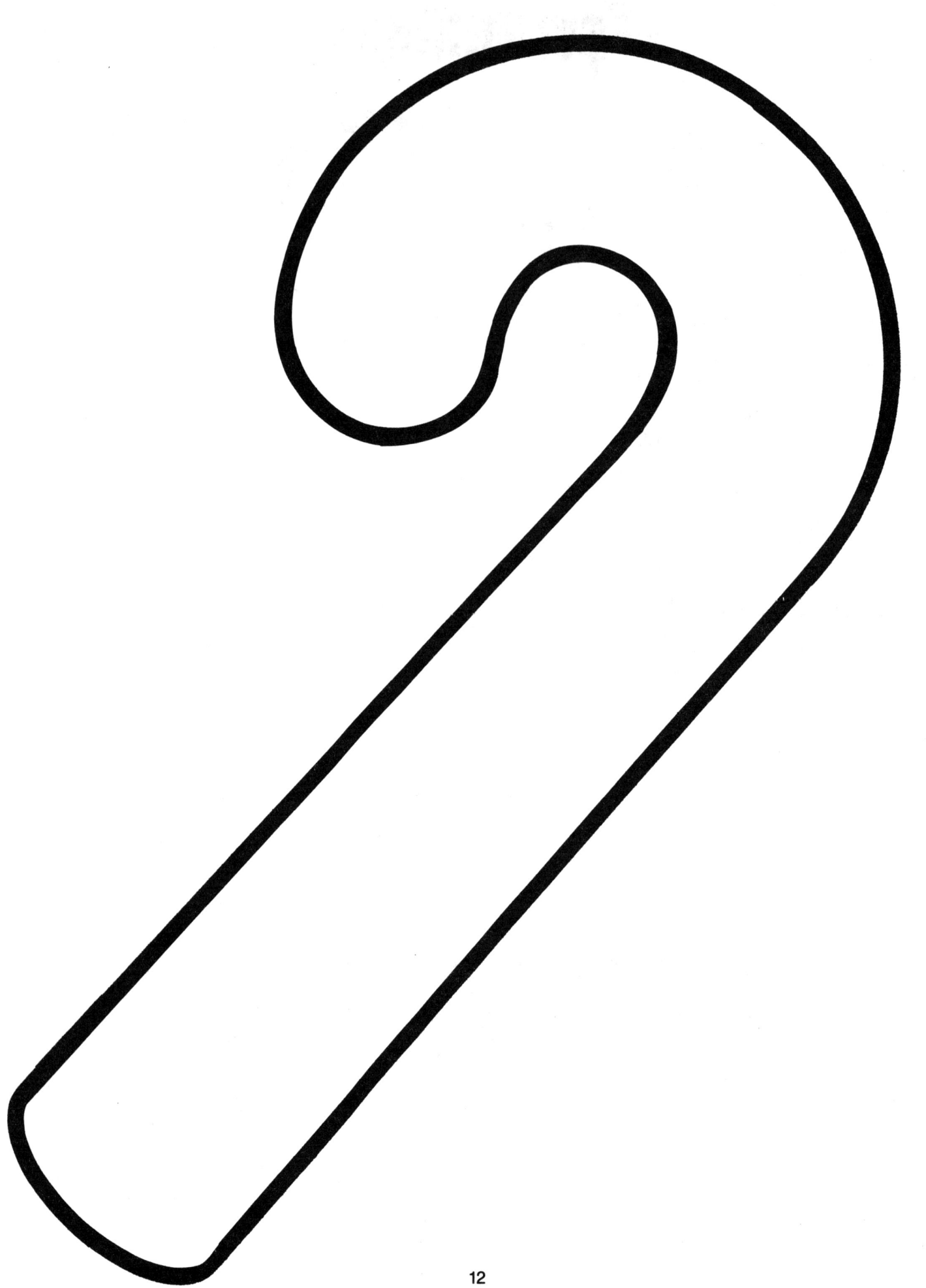

Candy Cane

Art: Reproduce candy cane pattern on white paper. Paint the stripes red and white. When the paint has dried, cut out around the outer edge. Children with more advanced motor skills can glue marshmallows and crumpled red tissue paper or red hot candies to create the candy cane stripes.

Sense adventures: Taste a candy cane. How does it taste? Can you describe it?

Number recognition, counting: Reproduce the candy cane pattern on white paper. Write a number in each stripe. Children practice counting and pointing to numbers as called out.

Categorizing: Buy candy canes and an assortment of mixed candies at the market. Place them in a pile. Ask the children to sort the candies by type, color and shape.

Letter sounds: Practice the hard sound of the letter "C" as heard in "candy cane." What other words can the children think of that begin with the same sound?

Problem solving: You are in school and a classmate brings in candy canes for the whole class. Your parents said you weren't supposed to eat candy. What should you do?

Wreath

Art: Crumple green tissue paper and glue it to the wreath pattern. Put a real red bow at the top.

Shape discovery: Use the wreath pattern to practice drawing circles. With a green crayon, make as many circles completely around the wreath as will fit. Then make small red circles to represent berries.

OR Use bottle tops dipped in paint to print the wreath with circles.

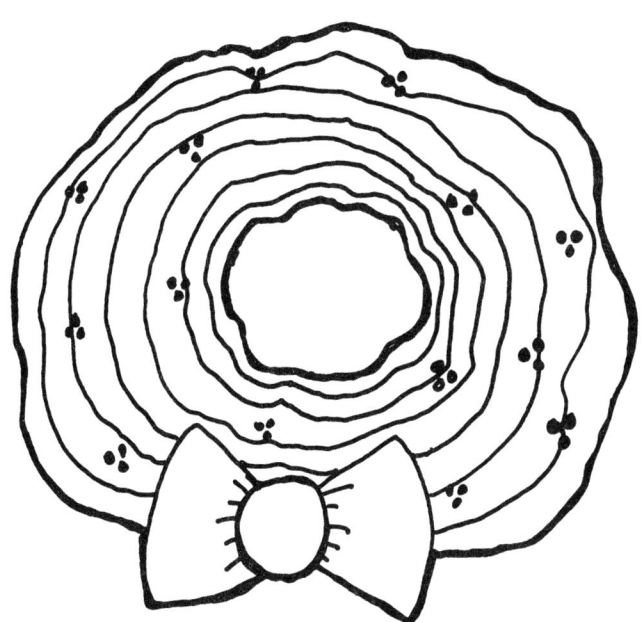

Small motor development: *Teacher task*—Cut several wreaths from heavy cardboard. The kids can now use these like frisbees. See if they can toss them and hit a target. How about trying to ring a holiday candle?

Movement: Make a human wreath. Join hands to make a large circle. Another group makes a smaller circle inside. Move to the right then move to the left. Ask one child to walk in a circle between the two human circles. Play holiday music while the children move in their human wreath.

Game time: Sit in a large circle. Play holiday music and pass a wreath around the circle. When the music stops the child holding the wreath will hold it up to his or her face like a frame and make a silly face. Start the music again!

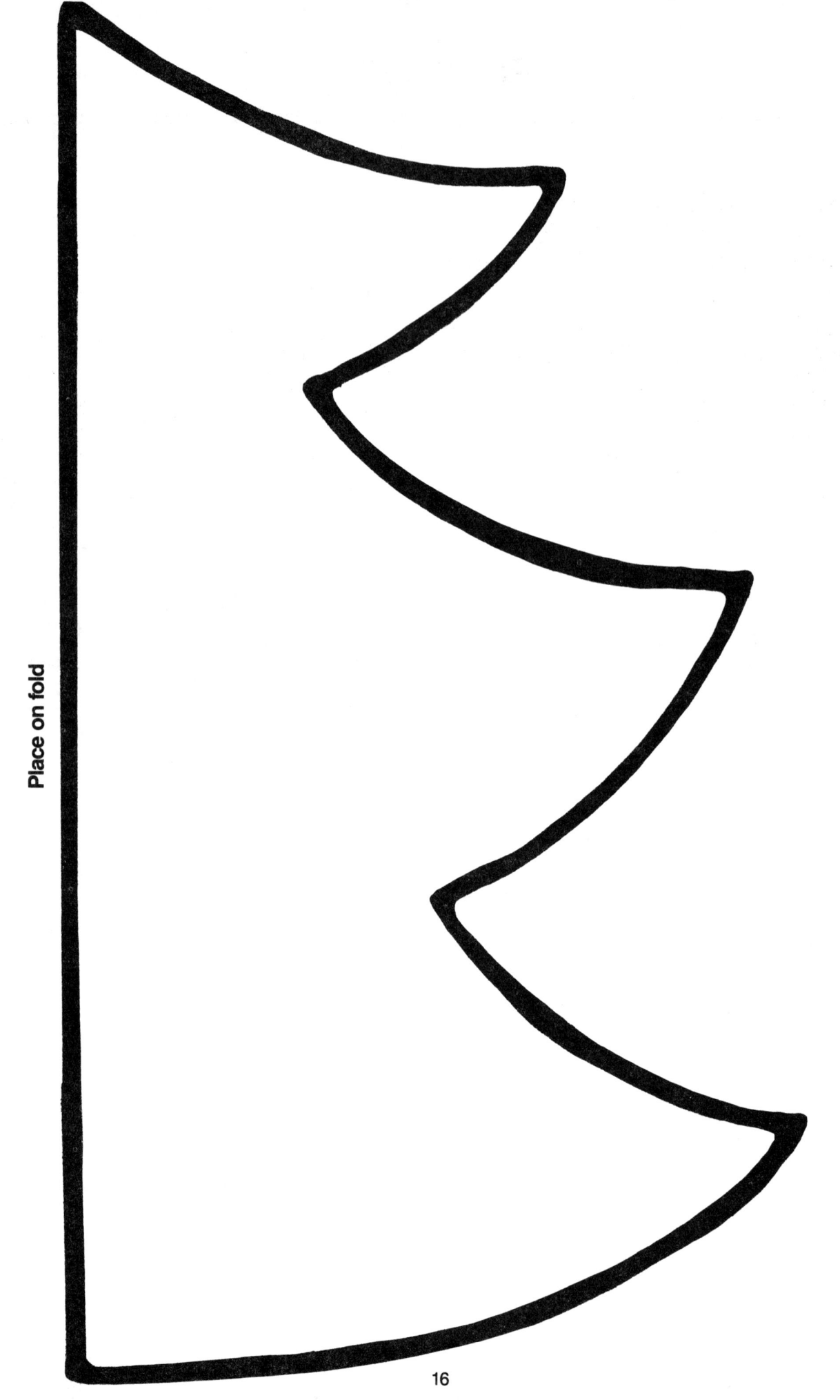

Christmas Tree

Art: Reproduce pattern. Trace onto green construction paper with straight side on fold as indicated. Cut out and open. Decorate with glitter, tinsel and paints.

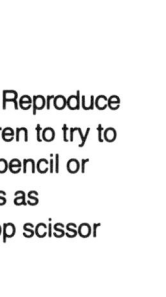

Small motor development: Reproduce the pattern on white drawing paper. Ask children to try to duplicate the zig-zag edge by drawing with a pencil or crayon next to the outline. Make as many lines as possible. Then try to cut on the lines to develop scissor skills.

Exploration and discovery: Take a walk around the school or through the neighborhood. How many different trees can you see? Try to bring back some samples if you can to make a classroom chart.

Sense adventures: Christmas trees are usually pine or spruce. They have a wonderful scent. Take turns smelling pine or spruce. Then try smelling other tree and flower samples.

Science: Bring a pinecone to share and study.

Counting: *Teacher task*—Using the pattern, cut a green felt tree. Cut colorful felt circles to resemble tree ornaments. Put the tree on the flannel board. Then ask children to come to the flannel board and put a specific number of ornaments on the tree.

Creative thinking: You are a gift under the Christmas tree. What are you?

Shapes: Cut a tree from the pattern and glue it to a larger piece of paper (or trace a tree onto white paper and color it in). Cut squares and rectangles to decorate as gifts and glue them under the tree.

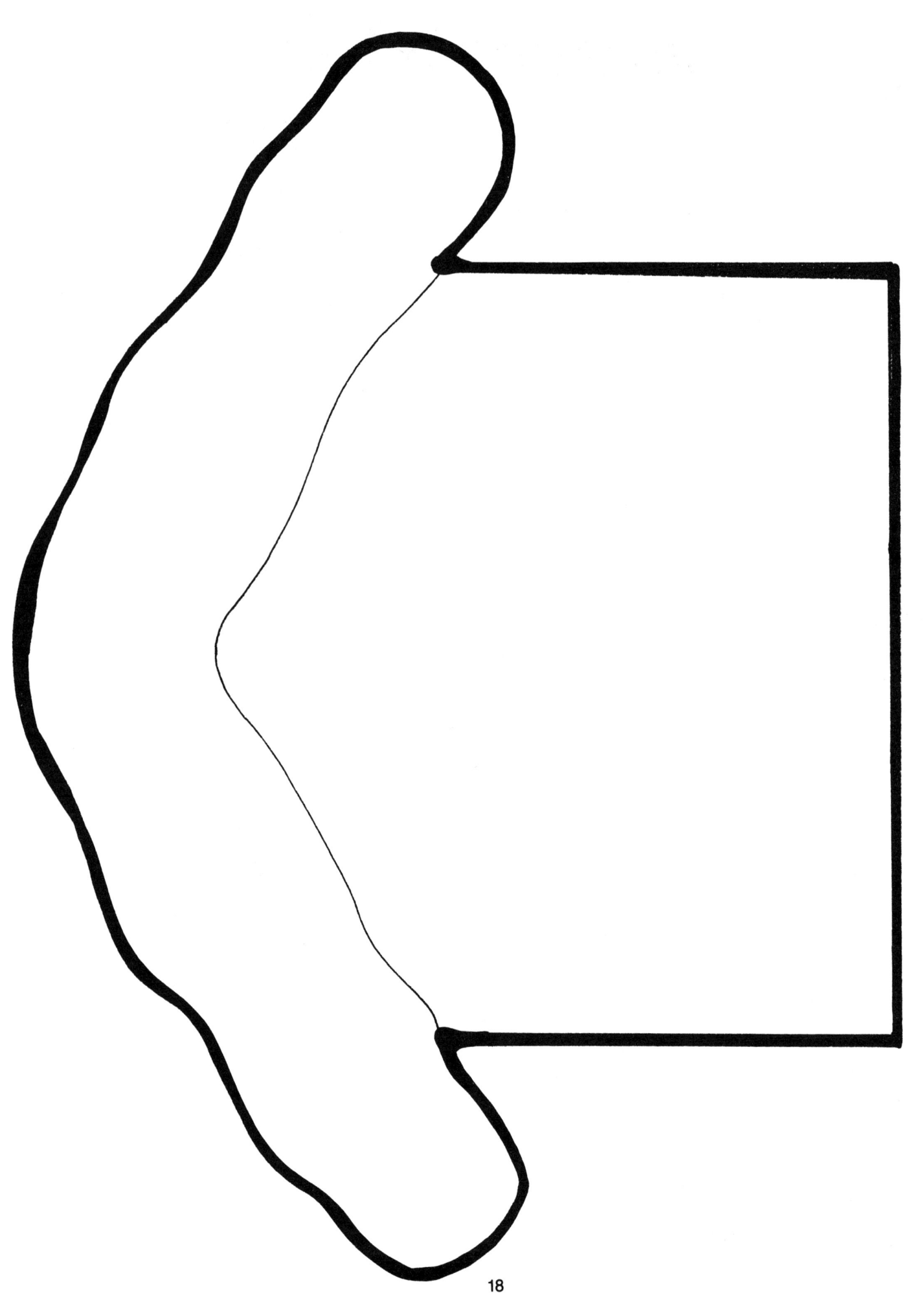

Gingerbread House

Art: Reproduce the gingerbread house pattern. Decorate with real icing and redhots.

Creative thinking: Who do you think lives in the gingerbread house? Tell a little about them.

Behavior modification: *Teacher task*—cut a gingerbread house for each child. Mount the houses to a bulletin board or a special spot in the classroom. Each time behavior deserves positive recognition, glue a gumdrop, candy cane or other wrapped candy to the house. The real reward is when the houses are taken down. Yum!

Cooking: Make real gingerbread. Then have a "party." Eat the gingerbread and use a gingerbread house as a placemat.

Categorizing: Gingerbread houses are covered with sweet treats. Pretend one was going to be covered with vegetables. What would we use? Now think of covering the house with fruits. Counts how many kinds of things in each category children can think of.

Critical thinking: What is a *real* house made from. How many things can the class list?

Game time: Go on a Hansel and Gretel search for a gingerbread house. Drop pieces of paper like a trail then ask a child to follow the trail, picking up paper scraps as he or she goes. There should be a house at the end of the trail. That child can now make a trail and ask another to follow it.

Bell

Use this bell pattern for both December holidays and January's New Year's Day to help ring in the new year.

Art: Reproduce pattern and cut out bell shape. Paint or color each bell. Crumple a piece of tin foil and glue it to the bell's clapper.

OR buy small bells at a craft or hobby shop and glue the bell to the clapper instead of tin foil.

Listening skills: Each child holds his or her bell. Teacher or leader calls out a child's name. When a child hears his or her name he "rings" his bell by shaking it in the air.

Game time: "Who rang the bell?" One child "It" sits with his or her back to the rest of the group. A bell is placed behind her back. One child is signaled to sneak up and ring the bell then sit down again quietly. On cue all children say "Who rang 'Its' name bell?" "It" turns around and has three chances to guess who rang the bell.

Rhyming: Recite the list below. When kids hear a word that rhymes with "bell" they ring their bells in the air. Read the list slowly allowing response time. The list can, of course, be added to if you wish.

me, go, well, sell, hop, up, can, small, smell, can, fell, girl, boy, dwell, fill, fix, quell, sip, gel.

Behavior modification: Hang a long piece of yarn on the wall. Using the pattern, cut bells from colored paper. Reward excellent classroom or behavior by hanging a bell on the yarn. Thank the children for their "bell-ringing behavior."

Counting: Count the number of bells on the award chair aloud each day either individually or as a group.

Oral expression: Talk about the new year and the expression "Ringing in the New Year." Then talk about other new year's expressions like "Turning over a new leaf" and "Father Time." Can they think of any other silly expressions?

Snowman

****

Art: Whip up a batch of Ivory snowflakes and pat them over the snowman. Add button nose and eyes.

Roleplaying: You are a snowman that came alive. What is the first thing you would say?

Music: Listen to the song "Frosty the Snowman." Pretend to be Frosty and dance to the music. You can help your snowman dance to the music too if the snowflakes have dried!

Nutrition: Make snowcones with crushed ice from a blender and fresh fruit juice. Kids can help use an ice cream scoop to put crushed ice in a cup. Then put juice over and eat with a spoon or straw.

Science: If you have snow outside your classroom, collect some. Make three snowballs, one large, one medium and one small. How long does it take each one to melt?

If you don't have snow outside your classroom, use crushed ice or ice cubes.

****

Dramatic play: Provide a box of hats, scarves, gloves, etc. and let kids dress up like snowmen. Can they stand just as still after they've dressed?

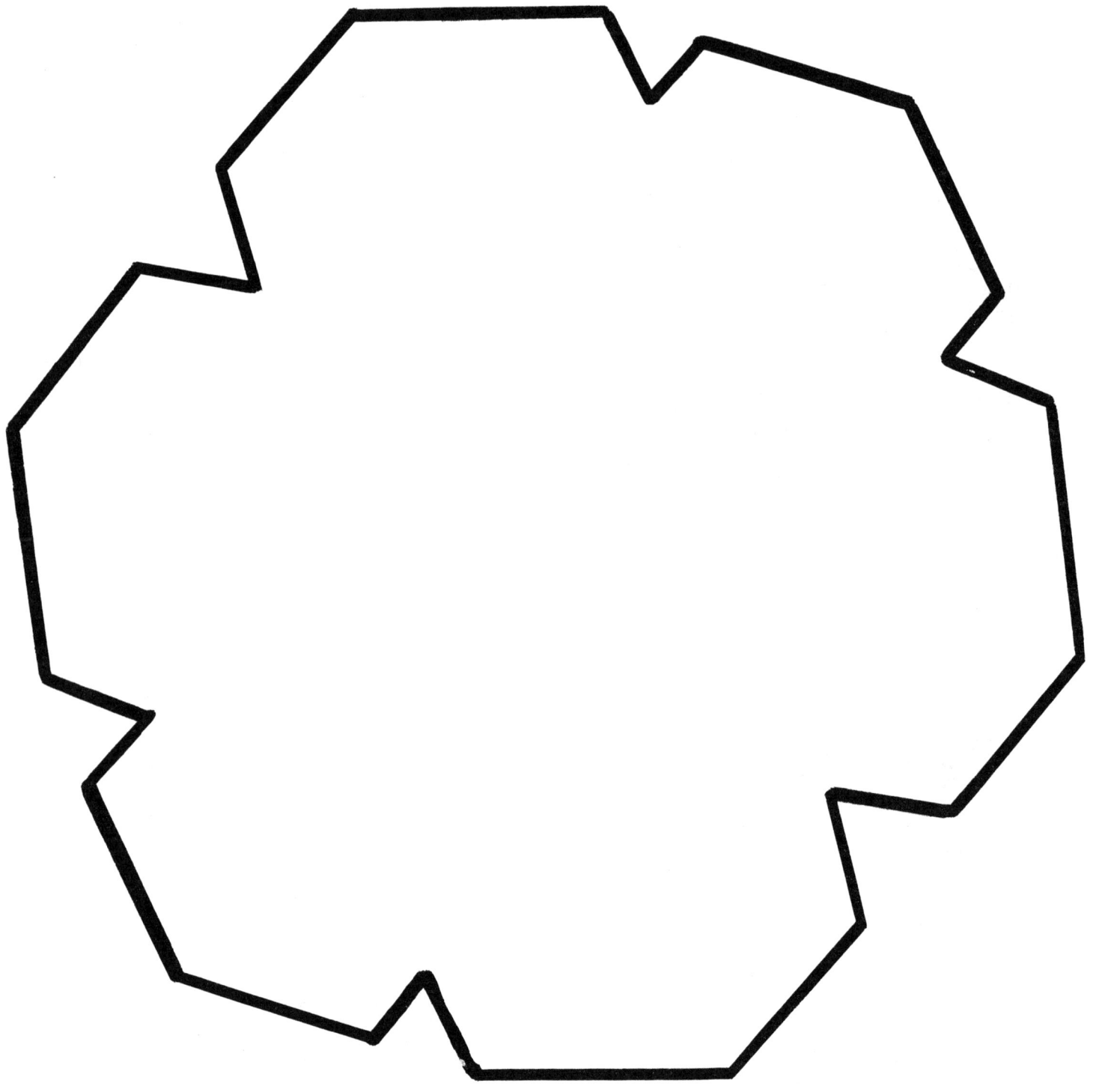

Snowflake

Art: Using the snowflake pattern, cut out a snowflake from white paper. Brush with glue and sprinkle with silver glitter or sugar. Carefully remove excess sugar or glitter.

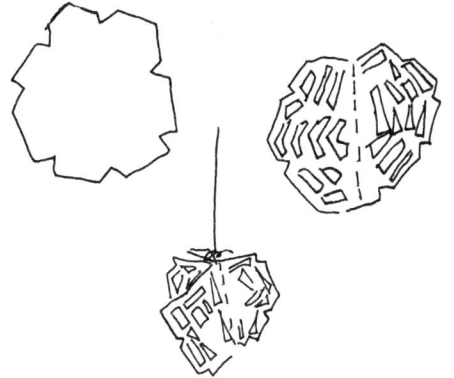

Here's another project for children with more advanced cutting skills: Cut out three white snowflakes. Fold each into quarters and cut out designs. Open, glue snowflakes, one on top of the other, down the center. When glue dries, the snowflakes can be gently folded at glue line to create a three-dimensional shape. Hang from the ceiling with thread.

Critical thinking: Look at the three-dimensional snowflakes that were cut. (If the children did not cut patterns in their flakes, make some samples to show.) No two snowflakes are the same. Discuss the fact that no two people are the same either. We are all different!

Creative thinking: What can you make out of snowflakes—snowman, snowball, etc. How would a snowflake feel on your tongue?

Game time: Play a cold version of "hot potato." Use the three-dimensional snowflake the children (or teacher) made to toss carefully around a circle. When the music stops, the child holding the snowflake is "frostbitten" and sits down. The game continues until just one child is left.

Science: What do people wear in different kinds of weather? How should we dress for the cold and snow?

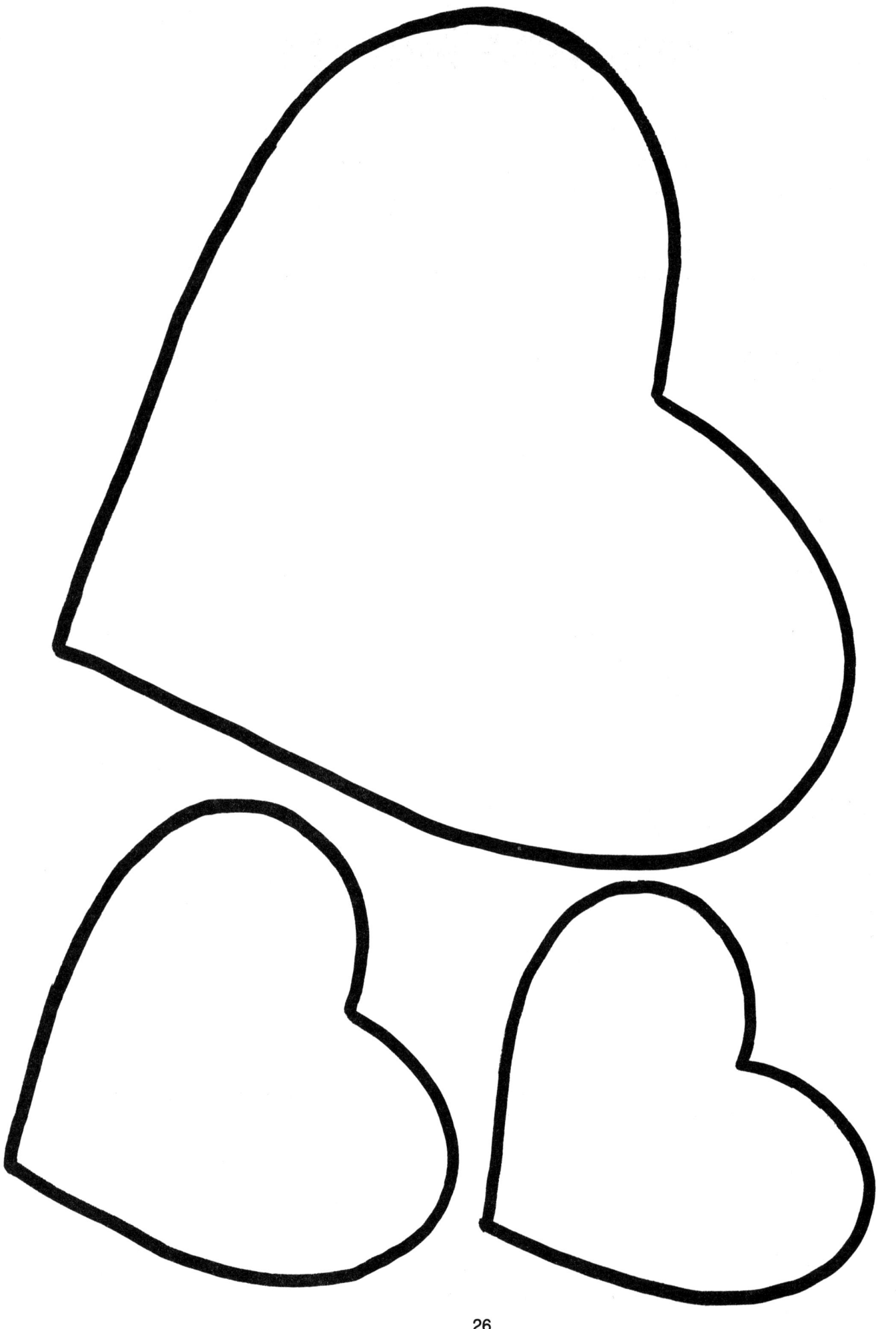

Valentine Hearts

Art: Cut out several heart patterns from different kinds of wrapping paper. Glue or paste hearts to white paper.

Comparing: Cut out all the hearts from red paper. Hold up the biggest. Glue onto paper, beginning with the largest on the left and ending with the smallest on the right.

Science: Where is your heart? Pin a paper heart on your clothing over your own heart.

Sense adventures: Put your hand over your heart. Can you feel your heartbeat? With a stethoscope, listen to your heartbeat. Can you tap each time you hear a beat? Jog in place. Now listen to your heartbeat. Is it different?

Language: Make a "love booklet." Cut six white paper hearts for each booklet. Decorate one heart for the cover. On the remaining hearts, write:
- I love _____ because _____
- Love makes me feel _____
- I love to eat _____
- The thing I love most to do is _____
- _____ loves me because _____

Children dictate love messages for each heart in their booklet.

Game time: *Teacher preparation* — Cut out several hearts. Cut each apart in a zig-zag pattern. Spread the hearts on a table. Can the children "mend" the broken hearts by matching them?

Shamrock

Art: Reproduce shamrock pattern on white construction or drawing paper. Provide watercolor or green tempera paint, thinned. Try to stay inside the lines!

Small motor development: Make a shamrock fan. Trace or reproduce pattern on green construction paper. Cut out. Glue the shamrock to a paint stirrer making sure the stirrer is glued from the top of the shamrock to the base to provide better stability. Practice fanning with the right hand then with the the left hand.

Vocabulary development: Use your shamrock fans to whip up some March winds! Listen carefully to the instruction. Be sure to match the fanning to the word descriptions.
- March winds are blowing. They're getting stronger. Now they're blowing harder!
- Now the wind is a gentle breeze. Feel it fan your face.
- Fan a friend with a light breeze.
- Look out! Hurricane winds! Thank goodness, the wind is finally gone!

About your world: The shamrock is the national flower of Ireland. Share pictures of Ireland. Find its location on a world map. Dance an Irish jig using the shamrock fans to encourage movement to the music.

Color recognition: Cut out green pictures from magazines. Glue them inside the shamrock shape.

Number recognition: *Teacher task*—cut a shamrock for each child. Write a number in each leaf—1, 2, 3 on one side of the shamrock, 4, 5, 6 on the other. Children sit with their shamrocks on the floor in front of them. Call out a number. Kids turn the shamrock so that the leaf with that number is directly in front of them.

Leprechaun Hat

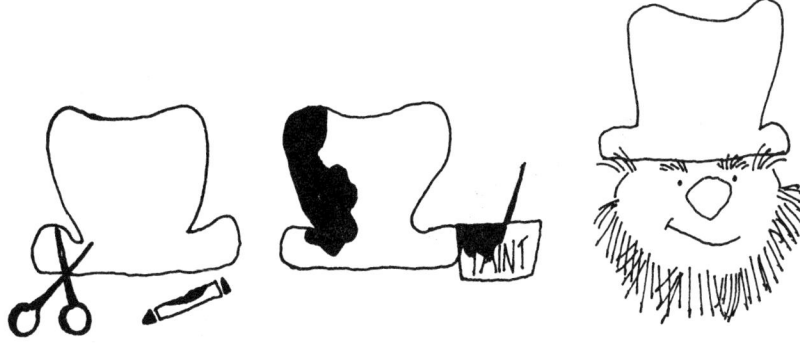

Art: Reproduce or cut out the pattern. Paint the hat (or reproduce on colored construction paper). Cut out a white paper circle or use a paper plate. Paint facial features, add yarn or fringed paper hair. Glue hat to leprechaun face.

Counting: Line up several children in a row. (They'll be wearing their hats, of course!) Ask the remaining children to count the "Leprechauns in a row." Change the row and count again.

Game time: It is thought that leprechauns may live under tiny mushrooms. Set up small cartons and let children leap over them. They will have fun and improve large motor skills!

Role playing: Cut out two hat patterns. Staple together at edges of hat brim. Children can wear their hats while they pretend to be leprechauns.

Critical thinking: A leprechaun can be good or mischievious. What good deeds could a leprechaun perform? What mischievious things could a leprechaun do? Make a list.

Behavior modification: Using the list as goals, be leprechauns for a day—but do only the good deeds!

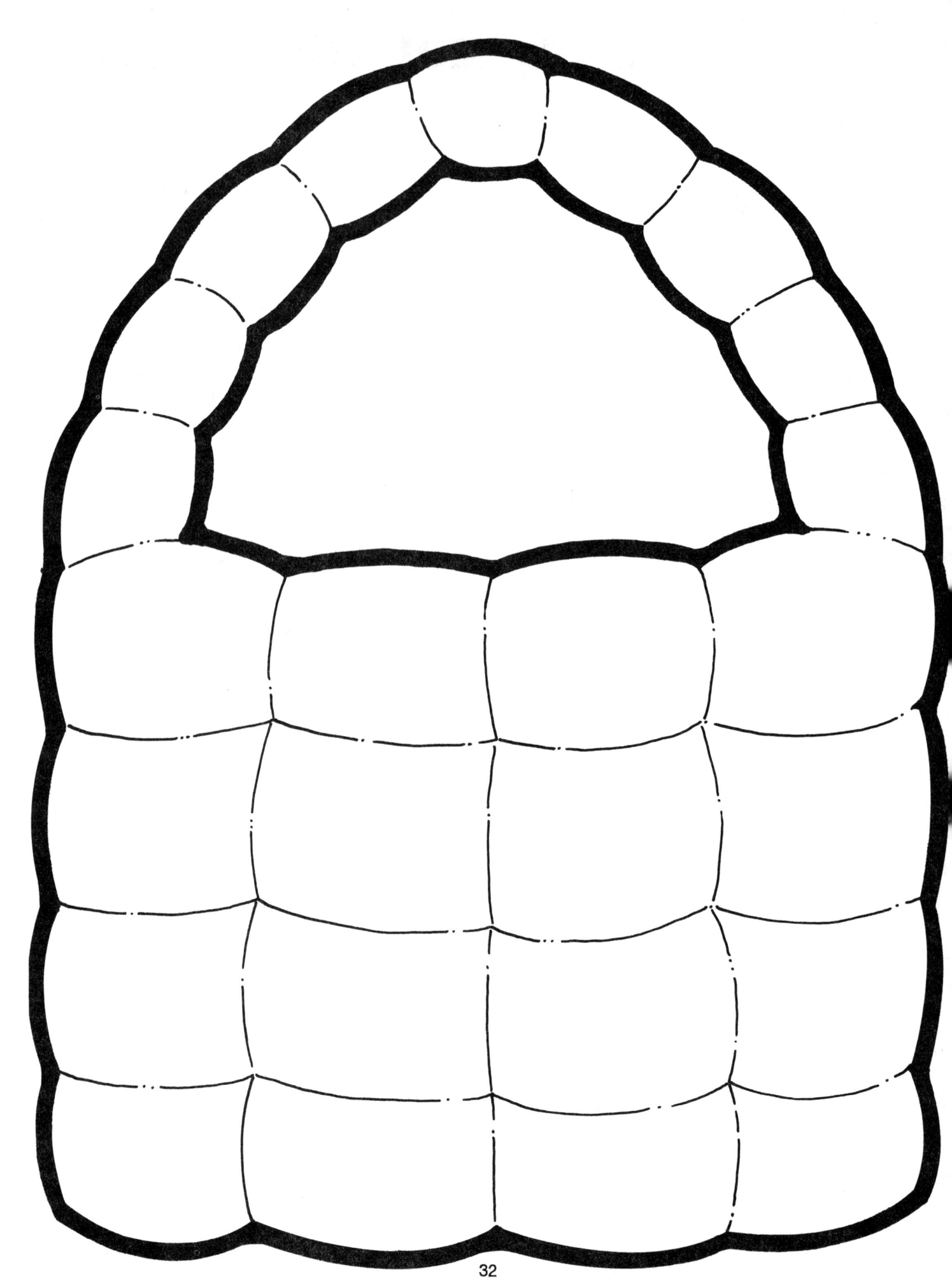

Basket

This pretty basket can be filled for Easter, May Day or Spring activities.

Art: Trace the pattern or reproduce on a larger sheet of paper. Use berry baskets to print the basket. Dip the baskets in paint and press onto pattern. When the paint has dried the basket can be filled depending on the holiday or season you are celebrating.
- Easter—blue colored eggs in and around
- May Day—Fingerpaint colorful flowers and leaves
- Spring—Glue magazine pictures of something you'd take on a picnic

Critical Thinking: Let's go on a picnic! What should we take?

Exploration and discovery: Plan a group picnic. Cut two baskets from the pattern and staple them together around the base, leaving the handle free. On picnic day, plan a nice walk and tuck a sandwich or surprise into each child's basket. At the picnic, kids can collect small stones and other items into their baskets to be shared and talked about upon returning to school.

Beginning letter sounds: *Teacher task*—Collect a variety of items (buttons, pencil, cup, etc.) and set them on a table next to a large basket. Ask children to find something that starts with the sound of the letter "B" (or any other letter) and put it in the basket. Be sure to make the sound for them if they are unfamiliar with letter sounds.

Memory development: Put some items in a basket. Show the basket to the kids. Let them look at the items for a minute or so. Then hide the basket. How many things can they remember and name?

Large motor development: Bring several baskets and nerf balls of varying sizes to class. Let children try to throw the ball into the basket. This can be played competitively if you wish.

Bunny

Art: Cut out the bunny pattern. Glue a soft cotton tail to one side and color eyes, nose, and whiskers on the other. Hang with yarn.

Sense adventures:

- Have you heard the expression "soft as a bunny?" Ask the children to bring in other things they can feel that are soft as a bunny.
- Bunnies have an excellent sense of smell. It seems they are always twitching their noses. Have children close their eyes and twitch their noses. Then hold something in front of them such as cinnamon, food extracts or coffee. Can they be super bunnies and identify the smells?

Exploration and discovery: Arrange to have a pet bunny in class. The children must be in charge of its care and cleaning.

Large motor development: Lay a bunny trail with yarn. Children can practice hopping down the bunny trail.

Right-left discrimination: Hold both arms over your head like floppy bunny ears. Listen to the directions and move your right ear then your left ear, then both.

Counting: *Teacher task*—Cut several colored eggs from construction paper. Ask a child to count a certain number of eggs. If the child is correct he or she gets to hide the eggs and the class hunts. Then it's another child's turn.

Role playing: You are the Easter bunny. You have run out of colored eggs. What will you do?

Egg

Art: Reproduce the pattern page on white drawing or construction paper. Color the egg heavily with crayon. Using a wide brush, wash pastel watercolors over the egg.

Role playing: Connect two eggs with yarn pieces long enough to fit over the head. Attach yarn to the sides of each egg so the egg can be tied front to back at each child's side. This will prevent the egg from falling away from the body. Now pretend to be an egg—you are boiling in a pot of water, you are being scrambled, you're frying in a pan and someone is turning you over, now you're sunnyside-up!

Dramatic play: You are an egg and your partner is a chicken. Have a conversation about what you see in the barnyard. Then reverse roles.

Creative thinking:: Cut an egg from the pattern. Then cut your egg in half using zig-zag cuts. What hatched from your egg? Glue the two parts onto paper and draw or find a magazine picture of what might have hatched from your egg.

Shapes: The egg is an oval shape. Cut other geometric shapes and glue them inside the egg. Take turns naming the different shapes.

Visual discrimination: *Teacher task*—Cut 5 eggs from the pattern. Cut each egg into 2 pieces. Spread the eggs on a table. Ask children to try and match the egg pieces as if they were doing a jigsaw puzzle. You may want to make several sets of eggs and store them in manila envelopes.

Small motor development: Let each child practice breaking an egg. First crack the shell on the side of a bowl then carefully pull the sections apart so the egg falls into a bowl. Then let everyone have a turn with a wire whisk and get the eggs ready to scramble in an electric frying pan. Have brunch for lunch!

Ice Cream Cone

Art: Cut out a cone from brown paper. Glue the cone to another piece of paper. Cut out circles from assorted colors of construction paper and glue to the top of the cone. Make a single scoop cone, or as many scoops as you like!

Counting: Use the flannel board scoops to practice counting the number of scoops on a cone. Change the number and let another child count.

Color recognition: *Teacher preparation* — Use the pattern to cut scoops from red, white, green and pink felt. Cut a brown felt cone and put it on the flannel board. Ask a child to help make an ice cream cone by putting on the red scoop. The next child will add another color and so on.

Sense Adventures: Place a drop of food extract on each scoop. Can the children identify the smell?

Critical thinking: Cut colored scoops from brown, pink, light green and white paper. What flavors could they be? (chocolate, strawberry, mint, vanilla)

Visual Discrimination: Bring in a sugar ice cream cone. Show the children the shape. Give each child a square piece of paper and ask them to try to make the cone shape from paper.

Talk-about time: What is your favorite flavor ice cream? How many different flavors can the class name?

Bow & Tie

After the children have had some classroom fun with their bows and ties turn the patterns into card decorations for Mother's Day and Father's Day!

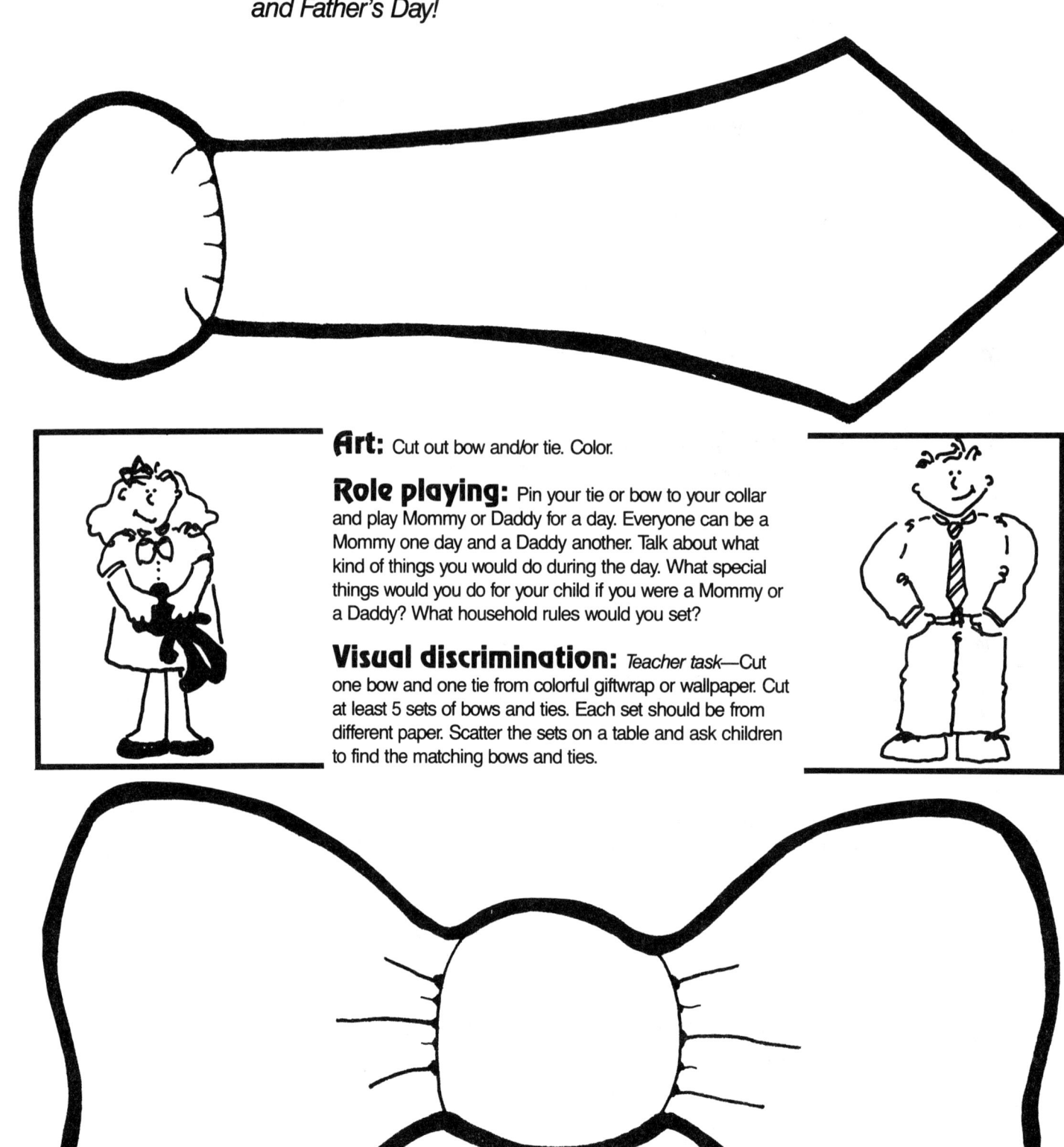

Art: Cut out bow and/or tie. Color.

Role playing: Pin your tie or bow to your collar and play Mommy or Daddy for a day. Everyone can be a Mommy one day and a Daddy another. Talk about what kind of things you would do during the day. What special things would you do for your child if you were a Mommy or a Daddy? What household rules would you set?

Visual discrimination: *Teacher task*—Cut one bow and one tie from colorful giftwrap or wallpaper. Cut at least 5 sets of bows and ties. Each set should be from different paper. Scatter the sets on a table and ask children to find the matching bows and ties.